Speed, Strength, and Stealth:

ANIMAL WEAPONS AND DEFENSES

BY JODY SULLIVAN RAKE

CONTENT CONSULTANT:
JACKIE GAI, DVM
ZOO AND EXOTIC ANIMAL VETERINARIAN

READING CONSULTANT:
BARBARA J. FOX
READING SPECIALIST
PROFESSOR EMERITUS
NORTH CAROLINA STATE UNIVERSITY

CAPSTONE PRESS
a capstone imprint

Blazers is published by Capstone Press,
1710 Roe Crest Drive, North Mankato, Minnesota 56003.
www.capstonepub.com

Books published by Capstone Press are manufactured with paper
containing at least 10 percent post-consumer waste.

Library of Congress Cataloging-in-Publication Data
Rake, Jody Sullivan.
    Speed, strength, and stealth : animal weapons and defenses / by Jody Sullivan Rake.
    p. cm. — (Blazers. Animal weapons and defenses)
    Includes bibliographical references and index.
    Summary: "Describes how animals use speed, strength, and stealth as weapons and
defenses"—Provided by publisher.
    ISBN 978-1-4296-6507-0 (library binding)
    ISBN 978-1-4296-8010-3 (paperback)
    1. Animal locomotion—Juvenile literature. 2. Physiology—Juvenile literature. I. Title.
II. Series.
QP301.R26 2012
591.5'7—dc23   2011034685

Editorial Credits
Mandy Robbins, editor; Kyle Grenz, designer; Svetlana Zhurkin, media researcher;
    Laura Manthe, production specialist

Photo Credits
Alamy: Dmitry Kobeza, 26–27, Photoshot Holdings, 24–25, Reinhard Dirscherl, 10–11, Rolf
Nussbaumer Photography, 8–9; Corbis: Michael & Patricia Fogden, 20–21, W. Perry Conway,
4–5; Dreamstime: Johannes Gerhardus Swanepoel, 22–23, Richard Lowthian, 16–17, Ryszard
Laskowski, 18–19; Getty Images: Bnsdeo, 14–15; National Geographic Stock: Ralph Lee Hopkins,
28–29; Shutterstock: David Dohnal, cover (bottom), Eric Gevaert, cover (top), Mark Bridger,
12–13, photobar, 6–7

Printed in the United States of America in
Stevens Point, Wisconsin.
102011   006404WZS12

TABLE OF CONTENTS

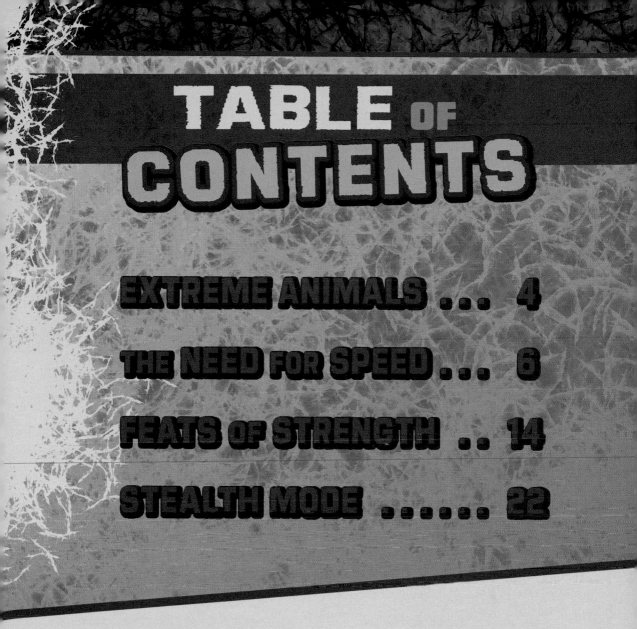

EXTREME ANIMALS

Extreme abilities help many animals survive in the wild. Speed, strength, and **stealth** are a few tricks animals use to hunt and escape the hunter.

stealth—the ability to move without being noticed

Using speed, stealth, and strength, a golden eagle sweeps a prairie dog off its feet.

THE *NEED* FOR SPEED

No land animal is faster than the cheetah. Cheetahs chase **prey** over African **grasslands**. They reach speeds of 70 miles (113 kilometers) per hour.

prey—an animal that is hunted by another animal for food

grassland—a large, open area where grass and low plants grow

Antelope are hunted by many **predators**. But they don't give up without a chase. The fastest antelope is the pronghorn. It runs up to 61 miles (98 km) per hour.

★ FIERCE FACT ★

Antelope can run for 30 minutes at high speed, while cheetahs tire in a few minutes.

PRONGHORN ANTELOPE

predator—an animal that hunts other animals for food

Sailfish grow up to 10 feet
(3 meters) long!

The fastest sea animal is the sailfish.
It zips through the water at speeds up
to 68 miles (109 km) per hour.

★ FIERCE FACT ★

A peregrine falcon's dives are called stoops.

The fastest animal of all is found in the sky. The peregrine falcon dives from great heights. It swoops down on prey while traveling more than 200 miles (322 km) per hour.

PEREGRINE FALCON

FEATS OF STRENGTH

Elephants are the world's largest land animals. A 12,000-pound (5,443-kilogram) elephant can carry up to 3,000 pounds (1,361 kg) on its back. That's equal to about 20 adult humans!

Eagles are the strongest birds. They often carry heavy prey in their **talons**. An eagle can carry up to four times its own weight.

☆ FIERCE FACT ☆

The strongest eagle is the African crowned eagle. It preys on monkeys and even small antelope.

BALD EAGLE

talon—an eagle's claw; a talon has four toes, each with a very sharp, curved nail

LEAFCUTTER ANTS

★ FIERCE FACT ★

Leafcutter ants use a combination of leaves and body fluids to create mold. The mold is food for the ants.

Ants are tiny but mighty.

They carry up to 50 times their size.

Ants carry leaves and bugs back to

the **colony**.

 colony—a large group of animals that live together

The rhinoceros beetle puts an ant to shame. It can carry 850 times its own weight. That would be like a human carrying two humpback whales!

A dung beetle can pull 1,141 times its own weight.

STEALTH MODE

Lions are stealth hunters. They crouch quietly in tall grass, unnoticed by prey. When the moment is right, they pounce with deadly force.

Female lions usually do most of the hunting.

The large surface of an owl's wings helps it fly with little flapping. Less flapping means less noise.

Owls are **nocturnal**. An owl's feathers and wings **muffle** sound as it flies. It quietly swoops down on prey.

nocturnal—active at night

muffle—to make a sound quieter

25

A crocodile will lie beneath the surface of the water. When a wildebeest walks up to take a drink, the crocodile snaps! It grabs its prey by the neck.

NILE CROCODILE

When a polar bear sneaks up on a land animal, the bear covers its black nose with a paw. Doing this helps the bear blend into the white snow.

Polar bears are patient hunters. A bear will wait for over an hour for a seal to emerge from its breathing hole. Their extreme patience allows for a sneaky attack.

GLOSSARY

colony (KAH-luh-nee)—a large group of animals that live together

grassland (GRASS-land)—a large, open area where grass and low plants grow

muffle (MUHF-uhl)—to make a sound quieter

nocturnal (nahk-TER-nuhl)—active at night

predator (PRED-uh-tur)—an animal that hunts other animals for food

prey (PRAY)—an animal that is hunted by another animal for food

stealth (STELTH)—the ability to move without being noticed

talon (TA-luhn)—an eagle's claw; a talon has four toes, each with a very sharp, curved nail

★ READ MORE ★

Doeden, Matt. *The World's Fastest Animals.* World's Top 10s. Mankato, Minn.: Capstone Press, 2007.

Landau, Elaine. *Owls: Hunters of the Night.* Animals After Dark. Berkeley Heights, N.J.: Enslow Publishers, Inc., 2008.

Murray, Julie. *Strongest Animals.* That's Wild! A Look at Animals. Edina, Minn.: Abdo Publishing, 2010.

INTERNET SITES

FactHound offers a safe, fun way to find Internet sites related to this book. All of the sites on FactHound have been researched by our staff.

Here's all you do:

Visit *www.facthound.com*

Type in this code: 9781429665070

INDEX